STAND UP AND LEAD

Kakudji K, Jose

Published by Kakudji K. Jose, 2024.

While every precaution has been taken in the preparation of this book, the publisher assumes no responsibility for errors or omissions, or for damages resulting from the use of the information contained herein.

STAND UP AND LEAD

First edition. November 24, 2024.

Copyright © 2024 Kakudji K, Jose.

ISBN: 979-8224393480

Written by Kakudji K, Jose.

Table of Contents

Introduction: Stand Up and Lead 1

Chapter 1: Stand Up and Lead! 2

Chapter 2: Good and Bad Leaders 5

Chapter 3: Behavior of a Leader 9

Chapter 4: Lead by Example 14

Chapter 5: Focus of a Good Leader 18

Chapter 6: Lead with Passion 23

Chapter 7: A Result of a Leader with a Pure Heart 28

Chapter 8: 10/10 Leaders Code: 10 Rules Leaders Must Apply to Be Great Leaders 34

Chapter 9: Lead with Passion 40

Chapter 10: A Result of a Leader with a Pure Heart 46

Chapter 11: The 10/10 Leader's Code: 10 Rules Leaders Must Apply to Be Great 52

Chapter 12: Lead with Passion 58

Chapter 13: A Result of a Leader with a Pure Heart 64

Chapter 14: 10/10 Leaders Code – 10 Rules Leaders Must Apply in Order to Be a Great Leader 70

Introduction: Stand Up and Lead

Leadership is the cornerstone of progress. It shapes nations, drives businesses, strengthens families, and transforms communities. Yet, leadership isn't reserved for a select few—it's a call to action for anyone willing to step forward, take responsibility, and inspire others.

At its heart, leadership is not about titles, positions, or accolades. It is about the impact you have on those around you. True leaders are those who recognize that their actions, decisions, and influence can shape the world in profound ways. They understand that leadership begins with self-mastery—knowing who you are, embracing your values, and committing to lead with integrity and purpose.

This book, *Stand Up and Lead*, is a journey into the essence of effective leadership. It is a guide for those who aspire to lead with courage, passion, and vision. Whether you are leading in your personal life, your community, or your career, this book will equip you with principles, tools, and insights to make a meaningful difference.

Through these pages, you will explore the traits of good and bad leaders, learn the behaviors that define true leadership, and discover the power of leading by example. You'll also delve into the importance of focus, passion, and a pure heart in leadership and gain practical wisdom from the **10 Rules of Great Leadership.**

Leadership is not a spectator sport—it requires action, resilience, and a willingness to learn and grow. So, take a step forward. Embrace the challenge. Stand up and lead. The world is waiting for leaders like you.

Chapter 1: Stand Up and Lead!

Leadership begins with a decision—a moment when you recognize the opportunity to make a difference and step forward. It's about refusing to stay on the sidelines and instead choosing to take responsibility, even in the face of uncertainty. To stand up and lead is to embrace the challenges, risks, and rewards that come with guiding others toward a shared vision.

What Does It Mean to Stand Up and Lead?

Standing up to lead isn't about being perfect; it's about being present. Leaders aren't born; they are made through their actions, choices, and persistence. The call to leadership comes in many forms—whether it's solving a problem in your community, driving a project at work, or supporting someone in need. The common thread is the willingness to act when others hesitate.

Why People Hesitate to Lead

Many hesitate to step into leadership roles because of:

- **Fear of failure**: Worrying about making mistakes or letting others down.

- **Lack of confidence**: Doubting their ability to lead effectively.

- **Uncertainty**: Not knowing where to start or how to navigate challenges.

- **Comfort zones**: Preferring stability over the responsibility leadership demands.

However, true leaders push past these doubts. They understand that growth happens when you take action despite fear and uncertainty.

The Mindset of a Leader

To stand up and lead, you need to cultivate a leader's mindset:

1. **Courage**: Leadership requires boldness. Courage isn't the absence of fear but the decision to act despite it.
2. **Vision**: Great leaders have a clear sense of purpose. They know where they are going and why it matters.
3. **Resilience**: Leadership is a journey filled with challenges. A resilient leader bounces back stronger from setbacks.
4. **Empathy**: Understanding and connecting with others is essential to inspire and motivate them.

Taking the First Step

Leadership doesn't require grand gestures—it starts with small, consistent actions. Here's how you can take your first steps:

• **Identify opportunities**: Look for areas where your skills and influence can create positive change.

• **Take responsibility**: Be willing to own your actions and decisions, even when they are difficult.

• **Learn and adapt**: Leadership is a continuous journey of growth. Seek knowledge, ask for feedback, and improve every day.

Inspiring Others to Stand Up

When you decide to lead, you inspire others to do the same. Leadership is contagious. Your courage and actions encourage those around you to believe in their own potential.

Call to Action

The first step in leadership is standing up. So, ask yourself:

- What challenge can I tackle today?

- How can I make a difference in my family, workplace, or community?

- What is stopping me from stepping forward?

Leadership is not a privilege of the few; it is the responsibility of anyone who cares enough to create change. Stand up. Take action. Lead with purpose.

Chapter 2: Good and Bad Leaders

Leadership is often defined by the results it produces, but it's also shaped by the way leaders influence those around them. Good leaders inspire, empower, and lead with integrity, while bad leaders often do the opposite—draining energy, creating division, and eroding trust. Understanding the difference between the two is essential to developing your own leadership style.

What Makes a Good Leader?

A good leader is someone who consistently demonstrates qualities that others respect and admire. They create an environment where people feel valued, motivated, and inspired to perform at their best.

Key Traits of a Good Leader:

1. **Integrity**: They do the right thing, even when no one is watching. Good leaders are trustworthy, transparent, and honest.
2. **Empathy**: They understand and care about the needs, emotions, and concerns of those they lead.
3. **Communication**: A good leader is an effective communicator. They listen actively, speak clearly, and ensure everyone is on the same page.
4. **Decisiveness**: They make tough decisions and take responsibility for them, even when they're unpopular.
5. **Vision**: Great leaders have a clear vision and can articulate it in a way that motivates others to work toward a common goal.
6. **Humility**: They are approachable, open to feedback, and quick to share credit with others.

A good leader isn't perfect—they make mistakes, face challenges, and have flaws. But they strive to grow, learn, and improve. Their focus is on helping others succeed, not just their own ambitions.

What Makes a Bad Leader?

Bad leadership, on the other hand, has a destructive effect on both individuals and organizations. Bad leaders prioritize their own success over the wellbeing of those they lead, and their actions often lead to poor morale, low engagement, and high turnover.

Key Traits of a Bad Leader:

1. **Self-centeredness**: Bad leaders put their own interests above those of their team. They are focused on their personal gain rather than the success of the group.
2. **Micromanagement**: They don't trust their team to get things done, constantly overseeing and controlling every decision, which stifles creativity and growth.
3. **Inconsistency**: Bad leaders often change their minds without explanation, which leads to confusion and frustration among their followers.
4. **Lack of Accountability**: They rarely admit when they're wrong and tend to blame others for mistakes.
5. **Poor Communication**: A bad leader struggles to communicate their ideas, leaving their team in the dark about goals, expectations, and progress.
6. **Arrogance**: They believe they know it all, disregarding the input or expertise of others.

The Consequences of Bad Leadership

Bad leadership doesn't just hurt the individual leader; it has wide-reaching effects on their followers and the organization. Here's what typically happens under bad leadership:

- **Decreased morale**: Employees or team members feel disillusioned and disconnected from their work.

- **Reduced productivity**: Without clear direction or support, people struggle to perform at their best.

- **High turnover**: Bad leadership leads to dissatisfaction, which can cause good employees to leave.

- **Toxic culture**: A bad leader often fosters a negative environment filled with distrust, fear, and lack of collaboration.

The Impact of Good Leadership

On the flip side, good leadership results in:

- **Empowerment**: People feel motivated to do their best work, knowing they have the support and trust of their leader.

- **Growth**: Both individuals and the organization as a whole experience continuous development and improvement.

- **Collaboration**: A good leader fosters a team-oriented culture where ideas are shared, and collective effort is prioritized.

- **Satisfaction**: When people feel valued and respected, they are more likely to remain engaged and loyal to their leader and organization.

How to Become a Good Leader

To become a good leader, reflect on the qualities you admire in others and strive to embody them yourself. Here are a few steps to improve your leadership skills:

1. **Commit to personal growth**: Always be willing to learn and evolve.
2. **Practice active listening**: Show your team that you care about their input and concerns.
3. **Lead with integrity**: Make decisions that align with your values, even when it's difficult.
4. **Provide support and empowerment**: Trust your team and give them the resources they need to succeed.
5. **Lead by example**: Demonstrate the behavior and attitude you expect from others.

Conclusion

Good leadership has a lasting impact on people, organizations, and society. It's about putting others first, leading with purpose, and constantly striving for growth. Bad leadership, in contrast, harms people and stifles potential. If you want to be a leader who makes a difference, commit to becoming the best version of yourself and lead by example.

Chapter 3: Behavior of a Leader

The behavior of a leader is what sets them apart from others. It's not enough to have a title or position—true leaders consistently exhibit behaviors that inspire trust, motivate others, and guide their teams toward success. Leadership is a reflection of how you act, the choices you make, and how you engage with those around you.

Key Behaviors That Define Great Leaders

1. **Consistency**
   Consistency is one of the cornerstones of effective leadership. A leader's behavior should align with their values, principles, and commitments, day in and day out. When a leader is consistent in their words and actions, they build trust with their team.

● **Why it matters**: Consistency helps others feel secure in their roles, as they know what to expect from their leader. It establishes a strong foundation for decision making and inspires loyalty.

● **How to practice it**: Ensure that your actions reflect your core values. Be predictable in your behavior, especially in high-stress situations.

1. **Emotional Intelligence**
   Emotional intelligence (EI) refers to the ability to recognize, understand, and manage your own emotions, as well as the emotions of others. Leaders with high EI are better equipped to build strong relationships, handle conflicts, and lead with empathy.

● **Why it matters**: Emotional intelligence is crucial in building rapport with your team, diffusing tense situations, and creating an environment of psychological safety.

● **How to practice it**: Work on developing self-awareness, managing your emotions, practicing active listening, and showing empathy toward others.

1. **Decisiveness**
    Great leaders don't hesitate when it's time to make a decision. They assess situations, consider their options, and take action with confidence. While not every decision will be perfect, a decisive leader can move their team forward by making choices and adjusting as necessary.

● **Why it matters**: Inaction and indecisiveness can create uncertainty, making it harder for teams to trust their leader. Decisiveness helps keep momentum going, even in difficult situations.

● **How to practice it**: Trust your instincts, gather the necessary information, and be willing to make decisions quickly. Don't let fear of failure hold you back.

1. **Accountability**
    Leaders who hold themselves accountable set an example for their teams. They take responsibility for their actions, acknowledge mistakes, and seek solutions rather than placing blame. Accountability fosters trust and shows that the leader is committed to improving.

● **Why it matters**: Accountability shows that leaders are willing to admit their mistakes, learn from them, and continuously improve. It encourages others to take ownership of their roles and responsibilities.

● **How to practice it**: Own your decisions—good or bad. If you make a mistake, take responsibility, learn from it, and share the lesson with your team.

1. **Adaptability**
   The world around us is constantly changing, and effective leaders need to be flexible and adaptable. Whether it's a shift in the market, a change in technology, or an unexpected challenge, leaders must be able to pivot and guide their teams through transitions.

● **Why it matters**: Adaptability allows leaders to respond to challenges with creativity and resilience. It helps leaders stay relevant and effective, even in the face of uncertainty.

● **How to practice it**: Stay open to new ideas, encourage innovation, and approach challenges as opportunities for growth.

1. **Inspiration**
   Leaders have the power to inspire others. Great leaders motivate their teams, spark creativity, and instill a sense of purpose in the work they do. An inspired team is one that is engaged, enthusiastic, and committed to achieving collective goals.

● **Why it matters**: Inspiration fuels passion, and passion drives productivity. A leader who inspires others creates a culture of excitement and commitment.

● **How to practice it**: Share your vision, recognize the hard work of your team, and celebrate milestones along the way. Create an environment where people feel excited about their work.

1. **Servant Leadership**

Servant leadership is the philosophy that the leader's primary role is to serve others. Instead of focusing on their own power or status, servant leaders prioritize the needs of their team, helping them grow and succeed.

- **Why it matters**: Servant leadership builds trust, encourages collaboration, and fosters a supportive culture where people feel valued.

- **How to practice it**: Support your team by providing resources, offering guidance, and removing obstacles. Show a genuine interest in the success and development of others.

The Impact of Leadership Behavior

Your behavior as a leader can either uplift or diminish your team. Positive behaviors like consistency, accountability, and emotional intelligence foster trust, unity, and productivity. Negative behaviors, such as dishonesty, micromanagement, and a lack of empathy, erode morale, create tension, and hinder progress.

How to Develop Strong Leadership Behaviors

Improving your leadership behavior is an ongoing process. Here are some steps to develop and strengthen these key behaviors:

1. **Seek Feedback**: Regularly ask for feedback from your team and peers to identify areas for improvement.
2. **Reflect on Your Actions**: Take time to reflect on your daily behavior and assess whether it aligns with your leadership values.
3. **Practice Self-Control**: Be mindful of your emotions, especially in high-pressure situations. Strive to remain calm and composed.

4. **Set a Positive Example**: Your team will follow your lead. Demonstrate the behavior you expect from others.

Conclusion

Leadership is defined by behavior. It's not enough to talk about the qualities of a great leader—you must embody them in your daily actions. By developing the behaviors of consistency, emotional intelligence, decisiveness, accountability, adaptability, inspiration, and servant leadership, you will build the foundation for trust, loyalty, and success in your team. Remember, your behavior speaks louder than your words.

Chapter 4: Lead by Example

One of the most powerful ways to lead is by setting the standard through your own actions. A leader who leads by example doesn't just talk about what should be done—they show others how to do it. Leadership is about modeling the behavior, work ethic, and attitudes you expect from your team. It's about demonstrating integrity, commitment, and passion in every action you take.

Why Leading by Example Matters

Leaders hold significant influence over their teams, and their actions often set the tone for the entire organization or group. When you lead by example, you not only earn the respect and trust of your team but also create a culture where everyone feels motivated to emulate the positive behaviors you display.

● **Builds trust**: People are more likely to trust and follow a leader who practices what they preach.

● **Creates accountability**: When you hold yourself to high standards, it encourages your team to do the same.

● **Fosters respect**: Leading by example shows that you are humble enough to do the work and commit to the same expectations as your team.

● **Inspires others**: Your actions will motivate others to act with the same level of excellence, responsibility, and passion.

Examples of Leading by Example

1. **Work Ethic**
   If you expect your team to work hard, be diligent, and meet deadlines, you must demonstrate those qualities yourself. A leader who consistently puts in the effort, meets deadlines, and shows dedication encourages the team to do the same.

● **Why it matters**: Your work ethic sets a benchmark. If you slack off, your team will follow suit. If you go above and beyond, they will likely feel motivated to match your effort.

● **How to practice it**: Lead by being punctual, prepared, and willing to put in the effort. Don't ask others to do something you're unwilling to do yourself.

1. **Integrity and Honesty**
   Integrity is perhaps the most essential trait for any leader. If you want others to be honest and ethical, you must demonstrate these behaviors first. Leading by example means being transparent, admitting mistakes, and doing the right thing even when it's hard.

● **Why it matters**: Leaders who lead with integrity build a culture of trust, respect, and accountability. When a leader shows honesty in their actions, it encourages their team to act with the same integrity.

● **How to practice it**: Be truthful in all your communications. If you make a mistake, own it and take steps to make it right. Uphold ethical standards in every decision you make.

1. **Commitment to Growth**
   A great leader is constantly growing and learning. Whether it's through reading, attending workshops, or seeking feedback,

showing your team that you're committed to personal and professional development encourages them to invest in their own growth.

- **Why it matters**: A commitment to learning demonstrates that leadership is a journey, not a destination. It sets a powerful example that learning never stops, and growth is always possible.

- **How to practice it**: Take the time to invest in your own education and self-improvement. Encourage your team to do the same by supporting them in their learning opportunities.

1. **Positivity and Resilience**
   Life and leadership are full of challenges. The way you handle adversity, stress, and setbacks influences how your team will approach their own challenges. A positive, resilient leader faces obstacles head-on, maintains a positive attitude, and keeps moving forward despite setbacks.

- **Why it matters**: When leaders display resilience and a positive attitude, it inspires their team to remain focused and motivated during difficult times.

- **How to practice it**: Stay optimistic, even in tough situations. Show your team that challenges are opportunities for growth. Embrace setbacks as part of the journey and maintain your commitment to the overall mission.

1. **Respect for Others**
   Leaders who treat everyone with respect, regardless of their position, create a culture of mutual respect. If you want your team to value and respect each other, it starts with you setting the tone. Treat every individual with kindness and fairness, and listen to their concerns.

- **Why it matters**: When leaders respect others, it fosters an environment where people feel valued, heard, and appreciated.

- **How to practice it**: Demonstrate respect in every interaction. Value diversity of thought, listen actively, and offer constructive feedback. Show appreciation for the contributions of everyone on your team.

The Power of Leading by Example in Difficult Times

It's during challenging times that your leadership truly shines. When things go wrong, the behavior you exhibit can either calm a storm or escalate the situation. Leading by example in tough times can inspire your team to stay strong, stay focused, and keep moving forward, no matter the obstacles.

- **Stay calm under pressure**: Your ability to remain composed can help diffuse tension and reassure your team.

- **Be proactive**: Take charge and find solutions, even when the path forward isn't clear.

- **Offer support**: Lead by offering help to those who may be struggling, whether emotionally, mentally, or professionally.

Conclusion

To lead by example is to align your actions with your values, setting a powerful and positive example for others to follow. It requires humility, consistency, and the courage to do what's right—even when it's difficult. When you lead by example, you inspire your team to adopt the same behaviors, creating a culture of trust, integrity, and mutual respect. The best leaders don't just tell others what to do—they show them how it's done.

Chapter 5: Focus of a Good Leader

A great leader is not only a visionary but also someone who understands where to direct their attention. A good leader's focus is sharp, purposeful, and strategic. They know what matters most to the success of their team and organization and make decisions accordingly. This focus enables them to guide their team with clarity and confidence, ensuring that everyone is aligned with the bigger picture.

The Importance of Focus in Leadership

Without focus, a leader can easily become distracted by minor issues, conflicts, or external pressures. In a fast-paced world, it's crucial for leaders to prioritize what truly matters and block out distractions that hinder progress. Leaders who maintain a clear focus can better navigate challenges, seize opportunities, and drive their team toward meaningful goals.

● **Creates alignment**: When a leader's focus is clear, it helps align the team's efforts toward a common goal, ensuring that everyone is working toward the same vision.

● **Promotes clarity**: A focused leader communicates priorities clearly, so the team knows what to concentrate on.

● **Maximizes impact**: Leaders who focus on what truly matters make a greater impact by concentrating resources, time, and energy on the most important tasks.

Key Areas Where a Good Leader Should Focus

1. **Vision and Direction**
   A good leader constantly keeps the vision in mind. They

understand that their role is to guide their team toward that vision, no matter how challenging it may seem. The focus on vision ensures that the team knows the destination and the route to take.

- **Why it matters**: A strong vision keeps everyone motivated and working toward a common purpose, even when the journey gets tough.

- **How to practice it**: Regularly remind your team of the long-term goals and values of the organization. Keep the vision visible and top of mind, ensuring it remains the compass that guides every decision.

1. **Team Development**
   An effective leader focuses on the growth and development of their team. Leaders are responsible for equipping their people with the skills, knowledge, and resources needed to succeed. Investing in team development fosters loyalty, builds expertise, and ensures that the team can tackle new challenges.

- **Why it matters**: A team that is constantly growing is more adaptable, engaged, and capable of achieving ambitious goals.

- **How to practice it**: Provide ongoing training, mentorship, and opportunities for personal and professional growth. Invest time in understanding the strengths and weaknesses of each team member to provide the right support.

1. **Building Relationships**
   Leadership is about people, and great leaders understand the importance of strong, authentic relationships. Whether with team members, peers, or external partners, a good leader spends time cultivating relationships built on trust and mutual respect.

- **Why it matters**: Strong relationships create a collaborative and supportive environment where people feel valued and understood.

- **How to practice it**: Be present, show empathy, and take the time to get to know your team. Foster open communication and actively listen to others. Make it a priority to build relationships both within and outside of the organization.

1. **Results and Accountability**
   While people and culture are critical, leaders also need to focus on results. A good leader ensures that the team remains accountable for achieving goals and meeting deadlines. They focus on driving performance and pushing the team to excel, while also recognizing and celebrating successes.

- **Why it matters**: Results are the measure of success. Without focus on performance, teams may struggle to achieve their objectives.

- **How to practice it**: Set clear expectations, monitor progress, and provide regular feedback. Hold yourself and your team accountable for meeting objectives and achieving results. Celebrate milestones to keep motivation high.

1. **Problem Solving and Innovation**
   Good leaders stay focused on solving problems creatively and encouraging innovation. They don't just focus on overcoming obstacles—they look for ways to turn challenges into opportunities for growth and improvement. A good leader is always looking for innovative solutions to complex problems.

- **Why it matters**: Focusing on innovation and problem-solving ensures that the team doesn't get stuck in the face of adversity. It opens the door to new opportunities.

● **How to practice it**: Encourage creative thinking and foster an environment where team members feel comfortable proposing new ideas. When a challenge arises, lead the team in brainstorming solutions rather than focusing on the problem.

How to Maintain Focus as a Leader

1. **Time Management**
   Effective leaders know how to manage their time. They prioritize tasks, delegate where appropriate, and avoid getting bogged down in insignificant details. Time management allows them to focus on the tasks that truly make a difference.

● **Why it matters**: Proper time management helps you allocate time to high-impact activities and avoid burnout.

● **How to practice it**: Use tools like calendars, to-do lists, or time-blocking to organize your day. Learn to say no to tasks that don't align with your goals or vision.

1. **Minimize Distractions**
   In a world full of distractions, staying focused requires intentional effort. A leader who constantly checks their email, engages in unproductive meetings, or becomes absorbed in minor issues can lose sight of what truly matters.

● **Why it matters**: Distractions pull your attention away from critical tasks, wasting time and energy.

● **How to practice it**: Limit distractions by setting clear boundaries, prioritizing high-value tasks, and delegating less important tasks. Find time in your day to focus deeply on key priorities without interruption.

1. **Delegate Effectively**

Leaders can't do everything themselves. Delegation is a key strategy for maintaining focus. By trusting others to handle certain responsibilities, a leader can focus their energy on areas where they can add the most value.

● **Why it matters**: Effective delegation empowers your team, builds trust, and allows you to concentrate on strategic leadership tasks.

● **How to practice it**: Identify tasks that can be handled by others and delegate them. Trust your team's abilities, and provide guidance as needed without micromanaging.

Conclusion

The ability to focus is what enables leaders to drive success. A good leader directs their attention to what matters most, ensuring that the team remains aligned, engaged, and motivated. By focusing on vision, team development, relationships, results, and innovation, a leader can build a thriving organization and create an environment where everyone is working toward a common purpose. Remember, leadership is not about doing everything yourself—it's about knowing where to focus and empowering your team to do the rest.

Chapter 6: Lead with Passion

Passion is the driving force behind great leadership. When leaders are genuinely passionate about their work, their team, and their vision, it creates an infectious energy that motivates and inspires others. Passion isn't something you can fake—it's a deep-rooted enthusiasm that guides decision-making, shapes interactions, and fuels resilience.

The Power of Passion in Leadership

A passionate leader doesn't just go through the motions; they live and breathe their mission. This passion shines through in their attitude, work ethic, and commitment to the cause. Passionate leaders inspire trust, loyalty, and a sense of purpose in those they lead. They make others believe in the vision and work tirelessly to bring it to life.

- **Inspires others**: Passion is contagious. When you lead with passion, your team will become excited and committed to the mission.

- **Creates a sense of purpose**: Passion helps people connect with their work on a deeper level, finding meaning in the everyday tasks.

- **Drives perseverance**: Passion helps leaders push through obstacles and challenges, maintaining enthusiasm even when faced with setbacks.

Why Passion is Essential for Leadership

1. **It Builds Commitment**
   When a leader is passionate about their work, it signals to the team that the mission is important. This level of commitment becomes a model for others, who in turn become more invested in the cause. Passion creates a ripple effect that drives collective commitment across the organization.

● **Why it matters**: A team that shares the leader's passion will work harder, put in extra effort, and stay motivated even during tough times.

● **How to practice it**: Share your vision, goals, and reasons for pursuing the work you do. Let your enthusiasm shine through your words and actions.

1. **It Boosts Morale**
   Leaders who lead with passion naturally uplift their teams. Their enthusiasm provides a boost of energy and excitement, making it easier for the team to stay engaged and positive, even when faced with challenges.

● **Why it matters**: Passionate leaders create a work environment where people feel inspired and energized to contribute their best.

● **How to practice it**: When challenges arise, remain enthusiastic and optimistic. Celebrate progress and remind your team of the bigger purpose behind the work they're doing.

1. **It Drives Innovation**
   Passionate leaders aren't afraid to think outside the box or explore new ideas. Their enthusiasm for the work motivates them to seek out innovative solutions, challenge the status quo, and continuously improve. Passionate leadership creates an environment where creativity and innovation thrive.

● **Why it matters**: Passionate leaders are more willing to take risks, explore new methods, and invest in new technologies—all of which lead to growth and innovation.

● **How to practice it**: Stay open to new ideas, encourage brainstorming sessions, and create a space where team members feel comfortable sharing their innovative solutions.

1. **It Creates Resilience**
   Leadership isn't without its challenges. There will be setbacks, failures, and moments of doubt. But a passionate leader has the resilience to push through these difficult times. Their love for their work and their commitment to the mission give them the strength to persevere.

● **Why it matters**: Passion fuels persistence. When things get tough, a passionate leader has the energy to keep moving forward, inspiring their team to do the same.

● **How to practice it**: Cultivate a mindset of perseverance. Remain positive and solution-oriented, even in the face of adversity. Show your team that challenges are an inevitable part of the journey and an opportunity to grow.

How to Cultivate Passion as a Leader

1. **Connect with Your Purpose**
   Passion starts with a strong sense of purpose. Leaders who are driven by a deep personal connection to their work are naturally more passionate. Reflect on what inspired you to pursue leadership and continually reconnect with that purpose to reignite your passion.

● **Why it matters**: When you understand why your work matters, it becomes easier to stay motivated and share that enthusiasm with others.

- **How to practice it**: Spend time reflecting on your mission and the impact you want to make. Revisit your goals regularly and stay connected to the bigger picture.

1. **Lead with Enthusiasm**
   Passion is often expressed through enthusiasm. Enthusiastic leaders show excitement and energy in everything they do. Their passion radiates, influencing their team's energy and attitude. Leading with enthusiasm shows your team that you believe in the work and the impact they are making.

- **Why it matters**: Enthusiasm is a visual and emotional expression of passion that inspires others to engage and invest in the work.

- **How to practice it**: Bring energy and enthusiasm into your interactions with your team. Show excitement for the work and for their contributions. Share your vision with enthusiasm, even when discussing routine tasks.

1. **Stay Curious and Open to Learning**
   Leaders who are passionate about their work are lifelong learners. They remain curious, seek new knowledge, and stay open to new experiences. By continuously learning, you keep your passion alive and inspire your team to do the same.

- **Why it matters**: Continuous learning fuels growth, development, and innovation, which are vital to maintaining passion and enthusiasm over the long term.

- **How to practice it**: Take part in professional development activities, read widely, and encourage your team to pursue their own learning goals. Embrace new ideas and approaches, and challenge yourself to grow.

1. **Surround Yourself with Like-Minded People**

Passion can be contagious, but so can negativity. Surrounding yourself with passionate, motivated individuals will amplify your own energy and commitment. A team that shares your passion for the work can help lift you up when you're feeling weary and encourage you to keep pushing forward.

• **Why it matters**: Surrounding yourself with a supportive, passionate team helps you maintain your own energy and keeps you focused on your mission.

• **How to practice it**: Build a team of individuals who are as passionate about the mission as you are. Engage with people who inspire you, challenge you, and encourage you to stay connected to your purpose.

Conclusion

Passion is the heart of leadership. It ignites a fire within the leader and creates a ripple effect that inspires, motivates, and drives the team toward success. Passionate leadership is contagious   it sparks creativity, fosters resilience, and creates a culture of excellence. If you want to lead with impact, it starts with leading with passion. Remember, a passionate leader doesn't just lead—they inspire, energize, and ignite the hearts of those they lead.

Chapter 7: A Result of a Leader with a Pure Heart

Great leadership begins within, and a leader with a pure heart brings out the best in others. A pure heart is one that is driven by genuine intentions, compassion, and a commitment to doing what is right, rather than seeking personal gain. Such leaders focus on the well-being of their team, the mission, and the greater good. When a leader leads with a pure heart, the results are transformative—not just for the organization but for the individuals they lead.

The Power of a Pure Heart in Leadership

A leader with a pure heart embodies integrity, honesty, empathy, and selflessness. These leaders inspire trust and loyalty because their actions are driven by noble principles, not by ego or selfish interests. The result of leading with a pure heart is that it fosters a culture of honesty, accountability, and mutual respect. It creates a safe environment where people feel valued and empowered to perform at their best.

- **Inspires trust**: Leaders who lead with integrity build strong relationships and a culture of trust.

- **Fosters loyalty**: People are more likely to stay committed to a leader who genuinely cares for their well-being.

- **Encourages selflessness**: Leaders with pure hearts encourage others to work together for the collective good, not individual gain.

Why a Pure Heart is Essential for Leadership

1. **It Builds Trust**

Trust is the cornerstone of any successful leadership. Leaders with a pure heart create environments where trust is easily built. They act with honesty, transparency, and fairness, which naturally cultivates strong relationships with their team. When trust is present, the team is more likely to follow, collaborate, and support the leader.

● **Why it matters**: A lack of trust undermines morale, productivity, and team cohesion. A leader with a pure heart establishes trust, making it easier to overcome challenges and work toward shared goals.

● **How to practice it**: Be honest and transparent in all your dealings. Keep your promises, communicate openly, and lead by example when it comes to integrity and trustworthiness.

1. **It Promotes Empathy and Compassion**
    A leader with a pure heart leads with empathy. They understand and care for the emotions, struggles, and challenges that their team members face. Such leaders take the time to listen, support, and encourage others, creating an environment where people feel cared for and understood.

● **Why it matters**: Empathy builds emotional connections that make the workplace a more supportive and collaborative environment. It also helps leaders make better decisions by considering the needs and feelings of others.

● **How to practice it**: Make time to listen to your team members' concerns, both professionally and personally. Show compassion when someone is struggling and offer support when needed. Lead with kindness and understanding, not just authority.

1. **It Strengthens Morality and Ethical Leadership**
    Leaders with pure hearts are grounded in strong moral values.

They make decisions based on what is right rather than what is easy or personally beneficial. This leads to ethical leadership that guides the organization with fairness, honesty, and a sense of justice.

● **Why it matters**: Moral leadership sets the tone for the entire team. Leaders who act with integrity instill a sense of right and wrong in others, creating a positive organizational culture.

● **How to practice it**: Make ethical decisions, even when no one is watching. Stand up for what is right, even if it's difficult or unpopular. Be willing to make sacrifices for the greater good.

1. **It Creates a Culture of Collaboration**
   Leaders who operate from a place of purity and selflessness encourage collaboration. They prioritize the needs of the team and the success of the group over individual achievement. This approach fosters an environment where people are willing to work together toward common goals and support one another along the way.

● **Why it matters**: A collaborative culture leads to higher morale, better communication, and more innovation. It helps teams overcome challenges by pooling their skills and knowledge.

● **How to practice it**: Encourage teamwork, acknowledge others' contributions, and create opportunities for everyone to collaborate. Celebrate team achievements and make sure credit is shared equally.

1. **It Promotes Long-Term Impact**
   Leaders with pure hearts make decisions that have a lasting positive impact. They focus not just on short-term gains but on the long-term well-being of their team, organization, and society. This approach ensures that their leadership has a lasting

legacy, rooted in kindness, integrity, and a commitment to making the world a better place.

● **Why it matters**: Short-term thinking may bring quick success, but it can lead to burnout, unethical behavior, or poor decision-making in the long run. Leaders with pure hearts focus on lasting success.

● **How to practice it**: Think long-term in your decision-making. Consider the ripple effects of your actions, and prioritize sustainability and positive impact over immediate results.

The Results of Leading with a Pure Heart

1. **Stronger Team Relationships**
   When a leader demonstrates care, trust, and integrity, they build strong relationships with their team. These relationships go beyond professional connections—they're rooted in mutual respect and shared values. This deep connection creates a loyal and committed team that will go the extra mile to achieve success.

● **Why it matters**: Strong relationships lead to high team morale, open communication, and a collaborative spirit.

● **How to practice it**: Invest in getting to know your team members on a personal level, acknowledge their contributions, and foster an environment of respect and trust.

1. **Greater Employee Satisfaction and Retention**
   Leaders who lead with a pure heart create workplaces where people feel valued and cared for. This results in higher levels of employee satisfaction and greater retention. People are more likely to stay in organizations where they feel supported,

appreciated, and aligned with the leadership.

- **Why it matters**: Employee turnover can be costly and disruptive. Leaders who treat their people well create an environment where employees are happy to stay and contribute.

- **How to practice it**: Make your team's well-being a priority. Offer support, recognition, and growth opportunities to keep morale high and retention strong.

1. **A Positive Organizational Reputation**
   Organizations led by leaders with pure hearts earn a reputation for integrity and ethical behavior. This reputation attracts like-minded people and opens doors to new opportunities, partnerships, and customers.

- **Why it matters**: A positive reputation leads to trust, loyalty, and business success. People are more likely to do business with organizations that prioritize ethics and integrity.

- **How to practice it**: Uphold ethical standards in all business practices. Communicate openly with stakeholders and always make decisions that align with your values and principles.

Conclusion

A leader with a pure heart creates a legacy that goes beyond profits and short-term success. The results of leading with integrity, empathy, and a focus on the greater good are powerful—stronger relationships, higher employee satisfaction, and a lasting positive impact on the organization. A pure-hearted leader inspires trust, fosters collaboration, and builds a culture where people feel valued and empowered. Leadership that comes from a pure heart isn't just about success—it's about making a meaningful difference in the lives of others and in the world around you.

Chapter 8: 10/10 Leaders Code: 10 Rules Leaders Must Apply to Be Great Leaders

Leadership is an art that requires a deep understanding of not only others but also oneself. It's not just about making decisions—it's about creating an environment where people feel seen, valued, and inspired to perform at their best. The most effective leaders follow a set of core principles that guide them through both the easy and the challenging times. These rules are the foundation of strong, influential leadership and can serve as a guide to those who aspire to lead with purpose and integrity.

In this chapter, we'll break down the 10/10 Leader's Code—essential rules every leader should embrace to build lasting success.

1. Lead by Example

As a leader, your actions speak louder than your words. The way you behave—your work ethic, attitude, and values—sets the tone for the entire team. Leaders who lead by example inspire others to follow suit and uphold the same standards. It's not enough to tell your team what to do; you must demonstrate the behavior you expect.

- **Why it matters**: People are more likely to adopt behaviors they see modeled by their leader. Leading by example builds trust and credibility.

- **How to practice it**: Show up on time, work with integrity, and maintain a positive attitude. Demonstrate the values you want your team to embody.

2. Be Transparent

Transparency in leadership means being open about decisions, processes, and challenges. When you are transparent, your team can trust you, and there's no room for gossip or misunderstanding. Honest communication builds confidence and helps everyone stay aligned.

- **Why it matters**: Transparency fosters trust and reduces confusion within the team. It also encourages open dialogue and feedback.

- **How to practice it**: Share both the good and bad news with your team. Explain the reasons behind decisions and invite questions to clarify any uncertainties.

3. Be Accountable

Accountability is one of the most important traits of a great leader. Owning your mistakes and learning from them sets a powerful example for others. When you take responsibility for your actions, it shows your team that accountability is a core value.

- **Why it matters**: Accountability ensures that everyone, including the leader, is responsible for their actions and decisions, promoting a culture of ownership and responsibility.

- **How to practice it**: Acknowledge mistakes and find solutions. Don't shift blame—take full responsibility and work to make things right.

4. Empower Others

Effective leaders empower their teams by trusting them with responsibilities, providing opportunities for growth, and encouraging their input. When people feel empowered, they take ownership of their work, show initiative, and perform at higher levels.

- **Why it matters**: Empowered team members feel more engaged, valued, and motivated. They are more likely to contribute their best ideas and efforts.

- **How to practice it**: Delegate tasks, provide guidance without micromanaging, and encourage your team to share their thoughts and ideas.

5. Be Compassionate

Compassion is a key aspect of emotional intelligence. A compassionate leader takes time to understand the feelings and challenges of their team. Leaders who show empathy create a supportive environment where people feel safe and respected.

- **Why it matters**: Compassion strengthens relationships and builds a loyal, cohesive team. It also improves morale and encourages individuals to be their best selves.

- **How to practice it**: Take an interest in your team's well-being. Listen actively when they share concerns, and offer support when needed.

6. Listen More Than You Speak

Great leaders are great listeners. They understand that leadership isn't just about giving orders; it's about hearing the voices of their team. Listening attentively builds rapport, fosters respect, and helps you gain insight into your team's needs and concerns.

- **Why it matters**: Listening helps you make informed decisions, shows respect for others' opinions, and encourages a culture of open communication.

• **How to practice it**: Make time for one-on-one conversations. Ask questions and genuinely listen to the answers. Avoid interrupting and focus on understanding, not just responding.

7. Keep Learning

Leaders who stop learning stop growing. Great leaders continually seek new knowledge, refine their skills, and challenge their own assumptions. The best leaders recognize that they don't have all the answers and are always striving to become better versions of themselves.

• **Why it matters**: Continuous learning keeps you adaptable, improves your leadership skills, and helps you stay relevant in an ever-changing world.

• **How to practice it**: Read books, attend seminars, seek mentorship, and invest in your own professional development. Encourage your team to also pursue their own learning opportunities.

8. Lead with Vision

Leaders must have a clear vision of where they want to go and how they plan to get there. A compelling vision helps your team see the bigger picture, aligns everyone's efforts, and drives motivation. Leaders who can communicate this vision clearly inspire others to follow.

• **Why it matters**: A strong vision gives your team purpose and direction. It helps them understand how their work contributes to the organization's larger goals.

• **How to practice it**: Communicate your vision clearly and frequently. Ensure that your actions align with the vision, and inspire others by helping them see their role in achieving it.

9. Stay Resilient

Leadership isn't always easy, and setbacks are inevitable. Resilient leaders bounce back from failure, adapt to challenges, and maintain focus on their long-term goals. Resilience in leadership fosters a "can-do" attitude in the team and sets the tone for overcoming obstacles.

- **Why it matters**: Resilience allows leaders to stay focused, positive, and effective even when faced with adversity. It sets an example for others to remain strong during tough times.

- **How to practice it**: When challenges arise, keep a positive mindset. Embrace failures as opportunities for growth and maintain focus on your ultimate goals.

10. Serve Others

True leadership is about serving others. The best leaders prioritize the needs of their team above their own. By adopting a servant leadership approach, leaders can foster a culture of collaboration, empathy, and respect.

- **Why it matters**: Servant leadership creates trust, promotes teamwork, and encourages employees to do their best because they feel valued.

- **How to practice it**: Lead with humility, be generous with praise, and always seek to help your team succeed. Put others' needs first and actively support their development.

Conclusion

The 10/10 Leader's Code isn't just a set of rules to follow—it's a way of being. Each of these principles forms the foundation of great leadership and empowers you to create a work environment that fosters growth, trust, and success. By following these rules, you'll not only enhance your leadership effectiveness but also inspire your team to achieve greatness.

Great leadership is about consistently demonstrating these principles. It's a journey of self-awareness, humility, and dedication. When you apply the 10/10 Leader's Code, you're setting the stage for success—not just for yourself, but for your team and organization as a whole.

Chapter 9: Lead with Passion

Passion is the fuel that drives great leadership. When leaders are passionate about their vision, mission, and the people they lead, they inspire and motivate others to give their best. Passion is contagious—it ignites energy, fosters commitment, and pushes individuals and teams to achieve extraordinary results. Without passion, leadership lacks the enthusiasm and drive needed to face challenges and persist through tough times.

In this chapter, we will explore the importance of leading with passion and how it can transform your leadership style, your team, and your results.

What Does It Mean to Lead with Passion?

Leading with passion means being deeply committed to your cause and purpose. Passionate leaders are emotionally invested in their goals and genuinely care about the success and well-being of their team. They wake up each day motivated to make a difference and inspire others to do the same.

- **Why it matters**: Passion brings energy and enthusiasm to everything you do. When you're passionate about your work, others will be inspired to follow you.

- **How to practice it**: Identify what excites you about your leadership role. Focus on the bigger picture and the impact your leadership can have. Let your passion shine through in your communication, actions, and decisions.

The Power of Passionate Leadership

1. **Inspires Others**
   When a leader is passionate, it's contagious. People are drawn to passionate leaders because they want to be part of something exciting and meaningful. Passionate leaders inspire others to share in their vision and work together to achieve common goals.

● **Why it matters**: Passion fuels motivation, and motivated people work harder, contribute more ideas, and stay committed to the mission.

● **How to practice it**: Share your enthusiasm with your team. Talk about your vision with excitement, and express your belief in their ability to make a difference.

1. **Increases Commitment**
   Passion is one of the key factors that increases commitment. Leaders who show passion for their work create an environment where people feel personally invested in the success of the team or organization. Passionate leaders can cultivate a sense of purpose among their team members, encouraging them to go above and beyond.

● **Why it matters**: When people are passionate about their work, they are more likely to stay engaged and work diligently to overcome obstacles.

● **How to practice it**: Help your team understand the deeper purpose behind their tasks. Show them how their contributions make a difference and keep the focus on the meaningful impact of their work.

1. **Drives Results**
   Passionate leaders drive results by setting ambitious goals and

pursuing them with relentless energy and determination. Their passion helps them to stay focused on the end goal and motivates the team to keep pushing, even when challenges arise.

● **Why it matters**: Passion is what keeps leaders and teams moving forward in the face of adversity. It sustains momentum and drives high performance.

● **How to practice it**: Set clear, inspiring goals that align with your passion. Encourage your team to remain focused and remind them of the bigger purpose when they face challenges.

1. **Fosters Creativity and Innovation**
    Passion for the work can spark creativity and innovation. Passionate leaders encourage their teams to think outside the box, explore new ideas, and push the boundaries of what's possible. The energy and enthusiasm that come with passion open the door to new ways of thinking and problem-solving.

● **Why it matters**: Creativity and innovation are essential for growth and progress. Passionate leadership fosters a culture of experimentation and continuous improvement.

● **How to practice it**: Create an environment where new ideas are welcomed. Encourage your team to take risks, explore different solutions, and share their creative thoughts without fear of failure.

1. **Helps Overcome Challenges**
    Challenges are inevitable, but passionate leaders have the resilience to face them head-on. Passion helps leaders maintain a positive attitude and determination when things aren't going well. Rather than giving up, passionate leaders see challenges as opportunities to grow and improve.

● **Why it matters**: Resilient leaders inspire their teams to push through difficulties and stay focused on the end goal. Passion gives the strength to overcome obstacles.

● **How to practice it**: Stay focused on your passion even in tough times. Encourage your team to maintain a positive attitude, find solutions, and keep pushing forward no matter how hard the journey becomes.

How to Cultivate Passion as a Leader

1. **Connect with Your Purpose**
   The most passionate leaders are those who have a deep connection to their purpose. Understanding why you lead and what you hope to accomplish gives you a sense of direction and motivation. Passion isn't something that happens overnight—it's a connection to the deeper purpose behind what you do.

● **Why it matters**: A clear purpose gives your leadership direction and makes the work feel meaningful. When your purpose is clear, passion flows naturally.

● **How to practice it**: Take time to reflect on your leadership journey and what inspires you. Ask yourself what impact you want to have on your team or organization. Let that purpose drive your passion.

1. **Lead with Energy**
   Energy is contagious. If you want your team to feel passionate about their work, you must bring energy to everything you do. Show enthusiasm for your work, your team, and the goals you're all striving to achieve. When you bring high energy, your

team will naturally respond with greater commitment and enthusiasm.

● **Why it matters**: Positive energy inspires and motivates others. A leader's energy can elevate the entire team's spirit and drive.

● **How to practice it**: Start each day with energy and enthusiasm. Find ways to energize yourself and your team—whether through small wins, recognition, or shared celebrations of success.

1. **Focus on What Excites You**
   Leadership can be demanding, but when you focus on what excites you, it becomes easier to remain passionate and engaged. Identify the aspects of leadership that truly inspire you and dedicate more time and effort to them. Passion naturally follows when you're working on things that bring you joy and fulfillment.

● **Why it matters**: When you focus on what excites you, you remain motivated and engaged. This enthusiasm translates into stronger leadership.

● **How to practice it**: Delegate tasks that drain your energy and focus on areas where you can make the most impact and where you feel energized. This ensures that your passion is channeled into areas that make the most difference.

1. **Inspire Others Through Action**
   Sometimes words aren't enough—leaders must show their passion through their actions. Lead by example and demonstrate your enthusiasm through your work ethic, commitment, and energy. Show your team that you're all in and excited about the journey ahead.

● **Why it matters**: Actions speak louder than words. When your team sees your passion in action, it ignites their own enthusiasm and commitment.

● **How to practice it**: Be hands-on when necessary. Dive into projects with your team, offer support, and show that you're fully invested in the mission. Your actions will inspire others to do the same.

Conclusion

Leading with passion isn't just about being enthusiastic—it's about being deeply connected to your purpose, motivated by your mission, and inspired to make a difference. Passionate leadership drives results, fosters innovation, and creates a team that is fully invested in the shared vision. When you lead with passion, you don't just get the best out of yourself—you bring out the best in everyone around you. Passion is the spark that ignites greatness, so always lead with it.

Chapter 10: A Result of a Leader with a Pure Heart

A leader with a pure heart is one who leads with sincerity, compassion, and authenticity. Their intentions are rooted in goodness, and they seek the well-being and success of others above all else. Leadership that comes from the heart is the kind that leaves a lasting impact, not just on the organization, but on the people who follow and support you.

In this chapter, we will explore what it means to lead with a pure heart, the results that come from such leadership, and how you can cultivate these qualities in yourself to become a leader who inspires genuine loyalty and respect.

What Does It Mean to Lead with a Pure Heart?

Leading with a pure heart means that your leadership is driven by a genuine desire to serve others and make a positive impact. Leaders with pure hearts are not motivated by selfish ambitions or personal gain; instead, they are guided by values like integrity, honesty, fairness, and a commitment to the greater good. They approach leadership with humility and compassion, always putting the needs of their team or organization first.

● **Why it matters**: Leaders who operate from a place of purity in their hearts create an environment of trust and respect. Their decisions are guided by what's best for the people they lead, which fosters a sense of unity and loyalty.

● **How to practice it**: Always check your motives. Ask yourself why you are leading and whether your actions are motivated by a genuine desire to help others. Stay true to your values and never compromise on them.

The Impact of Leading with a Pure Heart

1. **Builds Trust and Loyalty**
    Leaders with pure hearts naturally build trust within their teams. When people see that a leader is genuinely invested in their well-being, they feel safe and valued. Trust is the foundation of any strong team, and when you lead with authenticity and integrity, your team members will follow you with loyalty and commitment.

• **Why it matters**: Trust is essential for strong relationships and effective leadership. Without trust, even the most capable leader cannot inspire or motivate others.

• **How to practice it**: Be transparent, open, and honest with your team. Show vulnerability and acknowledge when you don't have all the answers. Trust your team to do their best and empower them to take ownership of their work.

1. **Creates a Culture of Collaboration and Respect**
    When a leader leads with a pure heart, they create an environment where people feel valued and respected. These leaders encourage collaboration, open communication, and mutual respect. People are more likely to contribute their ideas and skills when they feel they are working in a supportive and inclusive environment.

• **Why it matters**: A culture of collaboration and respect promotes creativity, innovation, and strong teamwork. When people feel safe and respected, they are more willing to contribute their best.

● **How to practice it**: Treat everyone with respect, regardless of their position or background. Encourage collaboration, celebrate diverse perspectives, and ensure that everyone's voice is heard.

1. **Promotes Ethical Decision-Making**
   Leaders with pure hearts make decisions based on ethics, fairness, and what is right, rather than on personal or organizational gain. They act with integrity and ensure that their decisions are aligned with the values they espouse. This ethical leadership fosters a sense of fairness and equality within the team, and it inspires others to adopt similar values in their own work.

● **Why it matters**: Ethical decision-making leads to sustainable success. It builds a strong reputation and cultivates respect, not just within the organization, but also in the broader community.

● **How to practice it**: Before making decisions, ask yourself if the choice is ethical and in alignment with your values. Consider the long-term impact of your decisions on others, and make choices that reflect integrity and fairness.

1. **Fosters Emotional Intelligence**
   Leaders with a pure heart are emotionally intelligent. They are aware of their own emotions, can manage them effectively, and are attuned to the emotions of others. This emotional intelligence allows them to build strong relationships, navigate conflicts with ease, and create a positive environment where people feel understood and valued.

● **Why it matters**: Emotional intelligence enhances communication, reduces conflicts, and improves team dynamics. Leaders who understand and manage emotions can foster a harmonious, high-performing team.

● **How to practice it**: Work on developing your emotional awareness. Practice empathy by putting yourself in others' shoes. Stay calm in difficult situations and learn to manage your own emotions to respond thoughtfully.

1. **Inspires Long-Term Success**
   When a leader leads with a pure heart, they inspire not only short-term success but also long-term sustainability. Leaders who prioritize the welfare of their teams, act with integrity, and make decisions with the long-term impact in mind, create an environment where success is both meaningful and enduring.

● **Why it matters**: Leaders who focus on long-term success create stability, foster growth, and build a lasting legacy. They ensure that their team or organization thrives not just today, but for many years to come.

● **How to practice it**: Focus on sustainable practices that benefit everyone in the long run. Encourage long-term planning and ensure that decisions are made with the future in mind.

How to Cultivate a Pure Heart in Leadership

1. **Practice Self-Reflection**
   Self-reflection is the cornerstone of a pure heart in leadership. Taking time to reflect on your own motivations, actions, and behaviors allows you to stay grounded in your values and intentions. Regular reflection helps you remain authentic and focused on what truly matters.

● **Why it matters**: Self-reflection allows you to remain in touch with your true self and avoid being swayed by external pressures or distractions. It keeps you aligned with your values and leadership purpose.

● **How to practice it**: Set aside time each day or week for reflection. Ask yourself tough questions about your leadership journey, such as "Am I leading with integrity?" or "Am I serving my team's best interests?"

1. **Lead with Humility**
    Humility is a key trait of leaders with a pure heart. Humble leaders are not focused on their own ego; they are more concerned with lifting others up. They give credit where it's due, acknowledge the contributions of others, and always remain open to feedback. Humility helps keep your leadership authentic and centered on others, not on yourself.

● **Why it matters**: Humility allows leaders to remain approachable, open-minded, and committed to continuous growth. It prevents arrogance and ensures that leaders serve others with a focus on the greater good.

● **How to practice it**: Recognize and appreciate the contributions of your team. Accept feedback graciously and never stop learning from others. Lead with the mindset that you are part of a larger team, not the sole focus of attention.

1. **Stay True to Your Values**
    Leadership with a pure heart requires a firm commitment to your values. Integrity, honesty, fairness, and kindness should be the foundation of all your decisions and actions. Leaders with pure hearts stay true to their values, no matter the circumstances or challenges they face.

● **Why it matters**: Staying true to your values helps you make decisions with confidence and ensures that you lead with authenticity. It fosters trust and respect and creates a positive culture within the organization.

● **How to practice it**: Know your core values and never compromise on them. When faced with tough decisions, reflect on your values to guide you. Let your values be the compass that steers your leadership.

51

Conclusion

A leader with a pure heart is a leader who inspires, nurtures, and builds lasting success. Leading with a pure heart means prioritizing others, acting with integrity, and staying true to your values. The results of such leadership are profound—strong relationships, ethical decisions, long-term success, and a positive organizational culture. By cultivating a pure heart, you not only become a better leader but also leave a lasting impact on those you lead.

Chapter 11: The 10/10 Leader's Code: 10 Rules Leaders Must Apply to Be Great

To be a great leader, it's essential to live by a set of guiding principles that drive your actions and decisions. These principles form the leader's code—rules that define how you lead, interact with others, and navigate challenges. Great leaders don't leave their values and priorities to chance; they intentionally apply a code of conduct that shapes their leadership. In this chapter, we'll outline the 10 essential rules every leader must follow to truly be great.

Rule 1: Lead with Integrity

Integrity is the cornerstone of effective leadership. A leader without integrity is a leader without trust. Leading with integrity means always doing the right thing, even when no one is watching. It's about being honest, transparent, and fair in all your dealings, and holding yourself accountable to the highest ethical standards.

- **Why it matters**: Integrity builds trust, and trust is the foundation of every great leader. Without trust, your ability to influence and lead effectively will be severely diminished.

- **How to practice it**: Be consistent in your actions and decisions. Don't compromise on honesty, even if it's difficult. Ensure that your behavior aligns with your values and that your team can always count on you to do what's right.

Rule 2: Always Lead by Example

Great leaders lead by example, setting the standard for others to follow. You must model the behavior you want to see in your team. Whether it's working hard, treating others with respect, or maintaining a positive attitude, your actions speak louder than your words.

● **Why it matters**: People are more likely to follow your example than just your instructions. Leading by example builds credibility and motivates your team to adopt the same standards.

● **How to practice it**: Be the first to show up, put in the effort, and embody the values you expect from others. If you want your team to perform at a high level, demonstrate that same level of commitment and excellence.

Rule 3: Communicate Clearly and Consistently

Communication is a key pillar of successful leadership. A great leader knows how to communicate their vision, expectations, and feedback clearly. They also ensure that their communication is consistent and open, making it easier for their team to align with goals and strategies.

● **Why it matters**: Miscommunication can lead to confusion, missed opportunities, and disengagement. Clear and consistent communication fosters collaboration and ensures everyone is on the same page.

● **How to practice it**: Be direct and transparent in your communication. Make sure your messages are clear, and encourage feedback from your team to ensure that they understand your vision and goals.

Rule 4: Stay Humble and Open to Feedback

Humility is an essential quality for great leadership. Leaders who stay humble recognize that they don't have all the answers, and they are open to feedback and learning from others. Being receptive to criticism and advice allows leaders to grow and improve continuously.

- **Why it matters**: Humble leaders earn the respect of their team and are seen as approachable. Feedback helps them grow, make better decisions, and strengthen their leadership skills.

- **How to practice it**: Encourage feedback from your team regularly, whether through formal reviews or informal conversations. Be open-minded and act on the feedback you receive to improve your leadership approach.

Rule 5: Empower Your Team

Great leaders know that they cannot succeed alone. They empower their team members by giving them the tools, trust, and responsibility to excel. Empowerment fosters independence, growth, and ownership among team members, which ultimately leads to greater success.

- **Why it matters**: Empowered teams are more engaged, productive, and loyal. When people feel trusted and valued, they are more likely to perform at their highest level.

- **How to practice it**: Delegate meaningful tasks, give your team autonomy, and support their development. Trust them to take ownership of their roles and provide them with the resources they need to succeed.

Rule 6: Maintain a Positive Attitude, Even in Adversity

Leadership requires resilience, and great leaders maintain a positive attitude even in tough situations. A leader's attitude has a direct impact on team morale, especially during difficult times. Staying positive, focused, and solutions-oriented helps your team stay motivated and confident.

● **Why it matters**: A positive attitude is contagious. When you remain optimistic, your team is more likely to stay motivated, solve problems, and keep pushing forward.

● **How to practice it**: Stay calm under pressure, focus on solutions rather than problems, and find opportunities in adversity. Encourage your team by acknowledging their efforts and maintaining a hopeful outlook.

Rule 7: Make Decisions with Clarity and Confidence

Leaders are called to make decisions, often in the face of uncertainty. The best leaders make decisions with clarity and confidence, knowing that their choices will guide their team forward. Making timely, well-considered decisions builds trust and sets a clear direction for your team.

● **Why it matters**: Indecision or lack of confidence can lead to confusion and delays. Clear, confident decision-making shows your team that you are in control and committed to the mission.

● **How to practice it**: Gather the necessary information, consult with your team when needed, and then make decisions with conviction. Trust your instincts and take responsibility for the outcomes.

Rule 8: Be Adaptable and Embrace Change

The world is constantly evolving, and great leaders understand the importance of adaptability. Whether it's adjusting to new technologies, shifting market demands, or changes in the team dynamic, a leader must be able to pivot and adjust their approach when necessary.

● **Why it matters**: Adaptability allows you to stay ahead of the curve and navigate change effectively. Leaders who resist change risk falling behind and losing relevance.

● **How to practice it**: Stay informed about industry trends and new technologies. Encourage innovation within your team, and be willing to adjust your strategies or plans when circumstances require it.

Rule 9: Prioritize the Development of Others

A great leader doesn't just focus on their own success—they also prioritize the development of those around them. By helping others grow, you create a cycle of continuous improvement and success. Leaders who invest in the development of their team build a culture of growth and achievement.

● **Why it matters**: When your team members grow, the entire organization benefits. Helping others achieve their potential creates a loyal, motivated team that will support you in your leadership journey.

● **How to practice it**: Identify growth opportunities for your team, such as training, mentorship, or new challenges. Provide regular feedback and support to help them reach their full potential.

Rule 10: Lead with Vision and Purpose

Great leaders are visionaries who know where they're going and inspire others to follow. A clear vision gives direction, purpose, and motivation. Leaders who communicate a compelling vision unite their teams around a common goal and drive them to achieve it with passion and commitment.

● **Why it matters**: Without a vision, teams lack direction and purpose. A clear vision helps align efforts and fosters a sense of shared mission.

● **How to practice it**: Clearly articulate your vision to your team, and ensure that every decision and action aligns with that vision. Inspire others by painting a picture of the future and showing them how their efforts contribute to achieving that vision.

Conclusion

The 10/10 Leader's Code is a roadmap for becoming a great leader—one who leads with integrity, inspires others, and drives results. These 10 rules are not just about achieving success in leadership, but about creating a positive, empowering environment where your team can thrive. Apply these principles consistently, and you'll find yourself not only becoming a more effective leader but also making a lasting impact on those you lead.

Chapter 12: Lead with Passion

Passion is the fuel that drives effective leadership. It is the energy, the enthusiasm, and the dedication that leaders bring to their roles every day. A leader who leads with passion doesn't just show up to do their job—they invest emotionally and mentally in the success of their team and the achievement of their goals. Passion is contagious, and when a leader is passionate about their mission, it inspires everyone around them to do their best work.

In this chapter, we'll explore what it means to lead with passion, how to harness that passion, and the tremendous impact it has on both the leader and their team.

What Does It Mean to Lead with Passion?

To lead with passion means to approach leadership with a deep commitment to your mission, values, and the people you lead. A passionate leader is someone who truly believes in what they are doing, and they show that belief through their words, actions, and decisions. Passion is not about superficial enthusiasm or fleeting excitement—it's about a deep, unwavering dedication to the cause and to those you serve.

- **Why it matters**: Passion in leadership is the spark that ignites motivation, creativity, and determination in others. When a leader is passionate, they inspire their team to push beyond their limits and strive for excellence.

- **How to practice it**: To lead with passion, take time to reflect on what drives you. Identify the values and causes that matter most to you, and incorporate those into your leadership approach. Share your passion with your team, and let your enthusiasm be a guiding force.

The Power of Passionate Leadership

1. **Inspires Others to Follow**
   When a leader is passionate, it inspires others to follow. Passionate leaders exude confidence and energy that others can't help but be drawn to. Their excitement is contagious, and their team feels compelled to contribute to the vision and mission with the same level of enthusiasm.

● **Why it matters**: Passionate leaders create a ripple effect that motivates everyone around them. When people see the fire in their leader's eyes, they want to be part of the journey and help make that vision a reality.

● **How to practice it**: Lead with enthusiasm, but stay grounded in your mission. Express your excitement and vision clearly, and encourage your team to contribute their own passion and energy to the cause.

1. **Boosts Team Morale**
   A leader's passion has a direct impact on team morale. When a leader shows up with passion, it uplifts the team, even during challenging times. Passionate leaders help their team stay motivated, positive, and focused on the end goal, even when obstacles arise.

● **Why it matters**: Passionate leadership boosts team morale by creating a sense of excitement and purpose. Teams are more likely to stay motivated, perform at a high level, and remain focused when their leader is passionate about the mission.

● **How to practice it**: Stay engaged with your team and show your enthusiasm, especially during tough times. Celebrate wins, no matter how small, and consistently remind your team of the bigger picture and why their work matters.

1. **Fuels Creativity and Innovation**
   Passionate leaders encourage creativity and innovation because they are not afraid to take risks or try new things. They are open to new ideas and approaches, and they inspire their team to think outside the box and come up with creative solutions to problems.

● **Why it matters**: Passionate leadership creates an environment where innovation can thrive. When people feel encouraged to express their ideas and take risks, they're more likely to contribute creative solutions and take initiative.

● **How to practice it**: Foster a culture of innovation by encouraging creative thinking, experimenting with new approaches, and celebrating the ideas that push boundaries. Show your team that you value their input and are excited to try new things together.

1. **Strengthens Commitment to the Vision**
   Passionate leaders have a strong, unwavering belief in their vision, and they communicate that vision with such conviction that others cannot help but get behind it. Passion helps to reinforce the leader's commitment to the mission and inspires others to commit to it as well.

● **Why it matters**: Passion strengthens the connection between the leader's vision and the team's actions. When a leader is deeply committed to the mission, that passion becomes contagious and aligns the entire team toward achieving the goal.

● **How to practice it**: Remind your team of the "why" behind what you're doing. Share your vision frequently and express how it drives you. Engage your team in the vision by showing them how their work contributes to achieving that larger purpose.

1. **Increases Resilience in Adversity**
   Passion gives leaders the strength to persevere in the face of challenges and setbacks. When things get tough, passionate leaders are able to remain focused, stay positive, and keep pushing forward, which motivates the team to do the same. Their passion provides the resilience needed to overcome obstacles and stay on course.

● **Why it matters**: Resilience is key to success. Passionate leaders are more likely to stay persistent and optimistic, even when things aren't going as planned. This resilience helps to inspire the team to stay focused on solutions, not problems.

● **How to practice it**: When facing challenges, keep your energy high, and remind your team of the long-term goals. Encourage them to keep going, share your optimism, and reinforce that setbacks are simply opportunities for growth.

How to Cultivate Passion in Leadership

1. **Conncct with Your Purpose**
   To lead with passion, it's crucial to be clear about your purpose. What drives you? What is the mission or cause that lights you up and inspires you to get out of bed each day? Take time to reflect on what excites you about your leadership journey and the impact you want to make.

● **Why it matters**: Passion is rooted in purpose. Leaders who are clear about their "why" are more likely to lead with energy and conviction.

● **How to practice it**: Reflect on your core values and the bigger picture. Revisit your mission regularly and align your daily actions with your long-term goals. Remind yourself of the impact you want to have.

1. **Engage with Your Team**
    Passion is best shared. When you engage with your team, you create a connection that allows your passion to flow naturally. Share your vision, your excitement, and your commitment with your team, and encourage them to bring their own passion to the table.

● **Why it matters**: Engaging with your team creates a sense of shared purpose and reinforces the passion behind the work.

● **How to practice it**: Have regular conversations with your team about the mission, the goals, and the progress. Encourage them to share their ideas and challenges. By connecting with them on a personal level, you'll inspire passion in return.

1. **Celebrate Progress and Successes**
    Passion grows when we see the fruits of our labor. Celebrating small wins, progress, and accomplishments reminds you and your team of why you're working so hard. Recognizing milestones fuels the fire and reinforces the belief that the work is worth it.

● **Why it matters**: Celebrating progress keeps the energy high and reinforces the value of the work being done.

● **How to practice it**: Acknowledge achievements publicly and privately. Celebrate when goals are met, and take time to reflect on the hard work that led to success. This keeps the passion flowing and motivates everyone to continue striving.

1. **Maintain a Growth Mindset**
    A passionate leader is always looking for ways to grow, both personally and professionally. Passionate leaders embrace learning opportunities, seek feedback, and strive to improve

themselves and their teams. A growth mindset keeps the energy and excitement alive.

- **Why it matters**: A growth mindset ensures that passion doesn't wane. It encourages continuous improvement and motivates you to keep learning and evolving as a leader.

- **How to practice it**: Stay open to learning new skills, techniques, and strategies. Encourage your team to take on new challenges and embrace change. Set a personal example by continuously seeking opportunities for self-improvement.

Conclusion

Leading with passion is one of the most powerful tools a leader can possess. It fuels motivation, drives commitment, and creates an environment where innovation and creativity thrive. Passionate leadership inspires teams to go above and beyond, and it makes even the toughest challenges seem surmountable. By connecting with your purpose, engaging with your team, and maintaining an unwavering commitment to the mission, you'll inspire those around you and create lasting success.

Chapter 13: A Result of a Leader with a Pure Heart

Leadership is not just about skills, strategies, or experience. At its core, it's about the heart—the purity of a leader's intentions and the genuine desire to serve and uplift others. A leader with a pure heart leads with sincerity, empathy, and compassion, prioritizing the well-being and growth of their team. This chapter explores the profound impact of leading with a pure heart, and how such leadership creates lasting results that benefit both the individual and the organization.

What Does It Mean to Lead with a Pure Heart?

Leading with a pure heart means having the right intentions behind every decision, action, and interaction. It means putting others first, striving to make decisions based on fairness and integrity, and always acting in a way that aligns with your values. A pure-hearted leader is motivated by the genuine desire to make a positive difference in the lives of those they lead, not by ego or personal gain.

- **Why it matters**: A leader with a pure heart fosters trust, loyalty, and respect among their team. People follow leaders they believe in, and purity of heart ensures that your leadership is both authentic and sustainable.

- **How to practice it**: Reflect regularly on your motivations. Ask yourself whether your decisions are truly in the best interest of your team, and whether your actions align with your core values. Always prioritize the well-being of others over personal gain or short-term success.

The Power of Leading with a Pure Heart

1. **Building Trust and Loyalty**
    Trust is the foundation of any successful relationship, and it is especially crucial in leadership. Leaders who lead with a pure heart build deep, authentic relationships with their team members. Their honesty, integrity, and care for others create a bond that goes beyond the transactional.

● **Why it matters**: When people trust their leader, they are more likely to be motivated, engaged, and loyal. Trust is a key ingredient in high-performing teams.

● **How to practice it**: Be consistent, honest, and transparent. Show genuine interest in the well-being of your team members, and always act with integrity. When people know you have their best interests at heart, they will be more likely to follow you and invest in your shared vision.

1. **Creating a Culture of Empathy and Compassion**
    A leader with a pure heart leads with empathy and compassion, understanding the challenges and struggles of their team members. This type of leadership creates an environment where people feel seen, heard, and valued, which strengthens team cohesion and morale.

● **Why it matters**: Empathy and compassion foster a sense of belonging and psychological safety. When team members feel understood and supported, they are more likely to collaborate and take risks without fear of judgment.

● **How to practice it**: Take the time to listen to your team, not just in terms of tasks and projects, but also their personal struggles and aspirations. Show that you care by offering support, encouragement, and understanding. Make your team feel safe to express their challenges and ideas.

1. **Inspiring Others to Do Good**
   Leaders with pure hearts inspire others to act with kindness, fairness, and honesty. Their example shows the power of leading with a selfless mindset, and they encourage others to lead in the same way. When a leader acts with integrity and goodwill, it creates a ripple effect throughout the organization.

● **Why it matters**: When leaders model positive behaviors, they inspire others to do the same. This leads to a culture of collaboration, respect, and ethical behavior throughout the team.

● **How to practice it**: Be intentional about modeling the behaviors you want to see in your team. Lead by example when it comes to kindness, generosity, and fairness. Encourage others to follow your example by acknowledging and celebrating acts of goodwill within the team.

1. **Making Decisions Based on Fairness and Integrity**
   Leaders with pure hearts make decisions that are fair, just, and rooted in their values. They are not swayed by personal interests, favoritism, or external pressure. Their decisions prioritize the collective well-being of the team, and they take into account the long-term impact on everyone involved.

● **Why it matters**: Fair and ethical decision-making ensures that everyone feels valued and respected. Leaders who make decisions based on integrity build a culture of fairness and justice, which increases team morale and reduces internal conflicts.

● **How to practice it**: Approach every decision with a sense of fairness. Consider all perspectives, and weigh the consequences of your choices carefully. Always ask yourself whether your decision reflects your core values and whether it benefits the team as a whole.

1. **Achieving Long-Term Success and Impact**
   Leaders with a pure heart achieve long-term success because their leadership is built on a foundation of trust, respect, and ethical behavior. Their authenticity and integrity create an environment where people are motivated to work toward shared goals. This results in sustainable success that benefits everyone, both personally and professionally.

● **Why it matters**: Success that is achieved through pure-hearted leadership is sustainable because it is built on trust and a positive culture. Leaders who focus on the long-term well-being of their team are more likely to achieve lasting impact.

● **How to practice it**: Focus on creating long-term value rather than seeking short-term rewards. Invest in your team's growth, prioritize their well-being, and make decisions that support sustainable success.

How to Cultivate a Pure Heart in Leadership

1. **Know Your Values and Align with Them**
   To lead with a pure heart, it's essential to be clear on your personal values. When you understand what truly matters to you, you can ensure that your leadership is aligned with these values. Being consistent in living out your values gives your leadership authenticity and credibility.

● **Why it matters**: Clear values provide a moral compass that guides your decisions and actions, ensuring they are always aligned with your higher purpose.

● **How to practice it**: Take time to reflect on your core values and principles. Make sure that your decisions, actions, and behavior reflect these values. When faced with difficult choices, ask yourself what your values would dictate.

1. **Practice Self-Reflection and Self-Awareness**
   Self-awareness is key to leading with a pure heart. By regularly reflecting on your actions, emotions, and motivations, you can ensure that you are leading authentically and not acting out of ego, fear, or insecurity.

● **Why it matters**: Self-awareness helps you stay true to your values and avoid being swayed by external pressures. It also helps you recognize areas for growth and improvement.

● **How to practice it**: Set aside time for regular self-reflection. Journaling, meditation, or discussions with a mentor can help you gain insight into your own leadership style and motivations.

1. **Be Transparent and Authentic**
   Authenticity is a key trait of a leader with a pure heart. Leaders who are open about their intentions, struggles, and decisions build trust and credibility. Being transparent allows your team to see the real you, which deepens their connection with you.

● **Why it matters**: Transparency fosters trust and allows your team to feel like they are part of the decision-making process. Authentic leaders are more relatable and earn respect.

● **How to practice it**: Be open about your intentions and challenges. Don't hide behind a façade or pretend to have all the answers. Share your thought processes with your team and let them know when you need support.

1. **Lead with Humility**
   Humility is an essential component of a pure heart. Leaders who are humble are not driven by pride or a desire for personal recognition. They recognize their limitations and are willing to learn from others. Humility allows leaders to serve their team without expecting anything in return.

● **Why it matters**: Humble leaders inspire trust and respect because they show that they value others' contributions. Humility also keeps leaders grounded and focused on the bigger picture.

● **How to practice it**: Acknowledge the contributions of others, and give credit where it's due. Be willing to admit when you're wrong or don't have all the answers. Focus on serving your team, rather than seeking recognition or praise.

Conclusion

Leading with a pure heart is the foundation for authentic, sustainable leadership. When your leadership is grounded in integrity, empathy, and selflessness, it creates a positive environment where trust, loyalty, and collaboration thrive. A leader with a pure heart inspires others to do good, make ethical decisions, and work toward the collective success of the team. By aligning your leadership with your values, practicing self-awareness, and leading with humility, you can achieve long-term success and create lasting impact, both within your team and in your personal journey.

Chapter 14: 10/10 Leaders Code – 10 Rules Leaders Must Apply in Order to Be a Great Leader

The journey of leadership requires a combination of skill, heart, and the ability to stay true to core principles. Just like any successful endeavor, there are rules or guidelines that, when followed, ensure a leader can navigate the complexities of leadership with purpose and effectiveness. In this chapter, we present the 10 rules that form the foundation of great leadership. These rules are timeless principles that, when consistently applied, will help you become a leader who inspires, empowers, and leads with integrity.

1. Lead by Example

The most effective leaders are those who practice what they preach. Leading by example means embodying the behaviors, values, and work ethic that you expect from your team. A leader who sets the standard through their own actions creates a culture of accountability and integrity.

• **Why it matters**: People are more likely to follow leaders who demonstrate the behavior they expect from others. Leading by example builds respect and trust, and it motivates others to emulate positive actions.

• **How to practice it**: Consistently align your actions with your words. Whether it's showing up on time, working hard, or maintaining a positive attitude, make sure your behavior reflects the standards you expect from your team.

2. Communicate Clearly and Effectively

Communication is a cornerstone of great leadership. Leaders must be able to convey their vision, goals, and expectations clearly and effectively. This includes listening actively, being open to feedback, and ensuring that messages are understood across all levels of the team.

- **Why it matters**: Clear communication ensures that everyone is aligned and working toward the same goals. It also reduces misunderstandings and prevents confusion, keeping the team moving in the right direction.

- **How to practice it**: Be clear and concise when giving instructions or sharing information. Encourage open dialogue with your team, and actively listen to their feedback and concerns. Use multiple forms of communication (e.g., meetings, emails, one-on-one conversations) to reach everyone.

3. Stay Humble and Open to Learning

A great leader knows that they don't have all the answers. Humility allows leaders to acknowledge their limitations and learn from others, including their team members. An open-minded leader is willing to seek advice, ask questions, and continually grow.

- **Why it matters**: Humility fosters trust and helps leaders avoid arrogance, which can create disconnects with their teams. It also allows for continuous improvement, which is crucial in a rapidly changing world.

- **How to practice it**: Seek feedback from your team, mentors, and peers. Acknowledge when you make mistakes, and view them as opportunities for growth. Stay curious and committed to learning new skills and knowledge.

4. Empower Your Team

A great leader understands that leadership is not about control but empowerment. Empowering your team means giving them the tools, resources, and autonomy they need to succeed. When people feel empowered, they take ownership of their work and are more motivated to achieve their goals.

● **Why it matters**: Empowered teams are more productive, innovative, and loyal. When team members feel trusted and supported, they are more confident in their abilities and take initiative.

● **How to practice it**: Delegate tasks and responsibilities that challenge your team members and allow them to grow. Provide the resources, training, and support they need to succeed. Trust them to make decisions and give them the freedom to innovate.

5. Maintain a Positive Attitude

A leader's attitude can set the tone for the entire team. A positive, optimistic attitude helps create an environment where challenges are seen as opportunities, and setbacks are viewed as stepping stones to success. Positive leadership fosters resilience, motivation, and a sense of possibility.

● **Why it matters**: A positive attitude is contagious. Leaders who maintain an optimistic outlook can inspire their teams, especially during difficult times. Positivity builds morale and keeps the team focused on solutions.

● **How to practice it**: Approach every situation with an optimistic mindset. Encourage your team to stay focused on the positive aspects of challenges and find solutions instead of dwelling on problems. Celebrate victories and frame setbacks as lessons to be learned.

6. Be Decisive and Take Action

Great leaders are decisive. They make informed decisions quickly and take action without hesitation. Indecision can paralyze a team and create uncertainty, so it's important for leaders to be clear and confident in their choices, while also being open to adjusting when necessary.

● **Why it matters**: Decisiveness builds trust and shows the team that you are confident in your leadership. It helps move projects forward and prevents stagnation.

● **How to practice it**: Gather the necessary information, weigh your options, and make a decision. Once a decision is made, act on it promptly. Trust your judgment, but also be flexible enough to adapt when circumstances change.

7. Build Strong Relationships

Leadership is not just about managing tasks but about building relationships. A great leader fosters strong, positive relationships with their team, colleagues, and stakeholders. Building trust and mutual respect creates a supportive environment that drives success.

● **Why it matters**: Strong relationships are the foundation of collaboration and team cohesion. They help to create a supportive environment where people feel valued and motivated to work together.

● **How to practice it**: Take time to get to know your team members as individuals. Show genuine interest in their well-being, ask about their goals, and offer support when needed. Cultivate a culture of respect, trust, and collaboration.

8. Act with Integrity

Integrity is one of the most important qualities of a great leader. Leaders must act ethically, uphold their values, and be honest in their dealings with others. Integrity builds trust and ensures that decisions are made in the best interest of the team and the organization.

● **Why it matters**: Integrity establishes credibility and trust. When people know they can count on you to do the right thing, they will respect you and follow you.

● **How to practice it**: Make decisions based on fairness, transparency, and honesty. Stand by your principles, even when faced with difficult choices. Lead with authenticity, and always prioritize what's best for the collective over personal gain.

9. Lead with Vision

A great leader has a clear vision for the future and communicates that vision effectively to their team. Visionary leaders inspire others by sharing their long-term goals and the purpose behind their efforts. A compelling vision provides direction and motivates everyone to work toward a common objective.

● **Why it matters**: A clear vision aligns the team and creates a sense of purpose. It helps everyone understand the bigger picture and why their contributions matter.

● **How to practice it**: Share your vision with your team regularly. Make sure everyone understands the overall goal and how their work contributes to it. Inspire them by showing the potential impact of their efforts.

10. Show Gratitude and Recognition

Acknowledging the contributions of others is a key leadership practice. Leaders who regularly express gratitude and recognize their team's efforts foster a culture of appreciation. Recognition motivates people to continue giving their best and reinforces positive behaviors.

- **Why it matters**: Showing gratitude and recognition boosts morale and increases job satisfaction. When people feel valued, they are more likely to be engaged, productive, and loyal.

- **How to practice it**: Celebrate milestones, achievements, and small wins. Thank your team members for their hard work, and give credit where it's due. Regularly acknowledge both individual and team contributions to maintain motivation.

Conclusion

The 10/10 Leaders Code is a blueprint for effective leadership. By leading by example, communicating clearly, staying humble, empowering your team, and maintaining a positive attitude, you will cultivate a leadership style that fosters growth, collaboration, and success. These rules are designed to help you build strong relationships, act with integrity, and inspire those around you to reach their fullest potential. Apply these principles consistently, and you will not only become a great leader but also inspire the leaders of tomorrow.